01

HOW MANY CROSSFITTERS DOES IT TAKE TO SCREW IN A LIGHTBULB?

Two—one to screw it in, and the other to film it for Instagram.

02

I TOLD MY FRIEND I STARTED CROSSFIT TO LOOK GOOD NAKED

I told my friend I started CrossFit to look good naked, but after my first week, I'm so sore I can't even undress without wincing.

03

WHAT'S THE DIFFERENCE BETWEEN A CROSSFIT GYM AND A PRISON?

In prison, they don't make you pay to do hard labor.

04

WHAT DO YOU CALL A CROSSFITTER WHO CAN'T DO HANDSTANDS?

An inverted extrovert.

05

CROSSFITTERS ARE LIKE SNOWFLAKES

CrossFitters are like snowflakes: unique, beautiful, and sometimes they melt under pressure.

06

CROSSFIT IS A LOT LIKE MARRIAGE

There's a lot of heavy lifting, and you're always trying to beat your previous performance.

07

THE FIRST RULE OF CROSSFIT IS:

Always talk about CrossFit.
The second rule is: Always talk about CrossFit.

08

CROSSFIT

Where the only thing more painful than the workouts is the price of membership.

09

WHAT DO YOU CALL A GROUP OF CROSSFITTERS AT A PARTY?

A "swole-mates" gathering.

10

CROSSFITTERS ARE LIKE A FINE WINE

They improve with age, until they start to whine about their knees.

11

WHY DID THE CROSSFITTER START USING A FOAM ROLLER AT WORK?

They heard it was a great way to work out all those "kinks" from their double unders!

12

CROSSFITTERS ARE LIKE VEGANS

You don't need to ask if they do CrossFit—they'll definitely tell you.

13

CROSSFIT WORKOUTS ARE LIKE A BOX OF CHOCOLATES

You never know when you're gonna puke.

14

I WAS SO BAD AT DOUBLE-UNDERS

That I accidentally turned them into a new CrossFit workout: the whip-yourself-into-shape challenge.

15

WHAT'S A CROSSFITTER'S IDEA OF A REST DAY?

Taking the stairs instead of the elevator.

16

WHY DO CROSSFITTERS LOVE HALLOWEEN?

Because they get to do "deadlifts" all night.

17

WHAT DO YOU CALL A GROUP OF CROSSFITTERS IN A HOT TUB?

A "swole-pool" party.

18

KNOCK, KNOCK.

Who's there?

Fran.

Fran who?

Fran-tically trying to finish this WOD, that's who!

19

CROSSFIT IS LIKE LEARNING TO RIDE A BIKE

Except the bike is on fire, and you're on fire, and everything is on fire because it's so intense.

20

CROSSFITTERS ALWAYS FINISH STRONG

Whether it's the last rep or the final moments in the bedroom.

21

IN CROSSFIT

The only thing more diverse than the workouts are the crazy socks people wear.

22

WHAT HAPPENED WHEN THE CROSSFITTER TRIED TO DO A TIRE FLIP IN THE PARKING LOT?

They accidentally flipped their own car.

23

CROSSFIT IS LIKE A CULT

But with more sweat and fewer robes.

24

CROSSFITTERS CAN'T WAIT FOR THE ZOMBIE APOCALYPSE

They've been training for it their whole lives.

25

WHAT'S A CROSSFITTER'S FAVORITE TYPE OF VACATION?

A "swole-cation" filled with workouts and protein shakes.

26

I THOUGHT I WAS READY FOR CROSSFIT

But then I met the Assault Bike and realized I wasn't prepared for that level of torture.

27

IN A PARALLEL UNIVERSE

There's a CrossFit gym where everyone skips leg day and focuses only on bicep curls.

28

KNOCK, KNOCK.

Who's there?

Squat.

Squat who?

Squat's the matter, can't handle another round?

29

HOW MANY CROSSFITTERS DOES IT TAKE TO CHANGE A LIGHTBULB?

One to change it, and five others to cheer them on and give high-fives.

30

CROSSFIT IS LIKE A ROLLERCOASTER

There's a lot of ups and downs, and you might throw up along the way.

31

CROSSFIT IS THE PERFECT WORKOUT FOR MILLENNIALS

It combines high intensity with a constant need for validation.

32

IF A CROSSFITTER DOES A WORKOUT AND DOESN'T POST ABOUT IT ON SOCIAL MEDIA

Did it really happen?

33

CROSSFIT IS LIKE SEX

Sweaty, intense, and you're always trying to beat your own personal record.

34

KNOCK, KNOCK.

Who's there?
Kipping.
Kipping who?
Kipping me up all night with your CrossFit stories!

35

WHY DO CROSSFITTERS HAVE SUCH GREAT SEX LIVES?

They know how to "push the pace" in more ways than one.

36

WHY DO CROSSFITTERS MAKE TERRIBLE SPIES?

They can't help but brag about their latest workout achievements.

37

A CROSSFITTER, A BODYBUILDER, AND A MARATHON RUNNER WALK INTO A BAR.

The CrossFitter says, "I can do more pull-ups than both of you combined." The bodybuilder replies, "Well, I can bench press more than both of you combined." The marathon runner chimes in, "That's cute, guys. I just ran a hundred miles for fun."

38

WHAT DO CROSSFITTERS AND PORN STARS HAVE IN COMMON?

They both know how to perform under pressure.

39

WHY DID THE CROSSFITTER WALK INTO A WALL?

They were too busy telling someone about their latest PR.

40

CROSSFIT IS LIKE A TRIP TO THE DENTIST

You know it's good for you, but that doesn't make it any less painful.

41

IF CROSSFITTERS WERE A SUPERHERO TEAM

They'd be called "The League of Extraordinarily Sore People."

42

WHY DID THE CROSSFITTER GO TO THERAPY?

They had a "Fran-ic" attack.

43

WHY DID THE CROSSFITTER LOVE THE WORKOUT "MURPH"?

He was great at giving them a run for their money.

44

KNOCK, KNOCK.

Who's there?

Angie.

Angie who?

Angie-one up for a hundred pull-ups, push-ups, sit-ups, and squats?

45

YOU KNOW YOU'RE A CROSSFITTER WHEN

You spend more time researching WODs than watching TV shows.

46

WHY DID THE CROSSFITTER FALL OFF THE PULL-UP BAR?

They were trying to explain the difference between "kipping" and "strict" mid-rep.

47

WHY DO CROSSFITTERS LOVE THE WORKOUT "HELEN"?

Because she's always there to give them a good run and lift their spirits.

48

CROSSFITTERS ARE ALWAYS LOOKING FOR A GOOD "CLEAN AND JERK,"

Whether it's at the gym or in the bedroom.

49

I THOUGHT I KNEW PAIN

But then I tried "Fight Gone Bad" and realized I had been living a lie.

50

WHY DO CROSSFITTERS LOVE ABBREVIATIONS?

Because they're all about efficiency—both in and out of the gym.

51

A CROSSFITTER GOES TO THE DOCTOR COMPLAINING OF EXTREME FATIGUE.

The doctor asks, "Have you been pushing yourself too hard at the gym?" The CrossFitter replies, "No, I've been doing the same number of AMRAPs, EMOMs, and HSPUs as always." The doctor shakes his head and says, "I think I've found the problem—you're speaking in CrossFit."

52

WHY DID THE CROSSFITTER ACCIDENTALLY THROW THEIR PROTEIN SHAKE ACROSS THE ROOM?

They were practicing their "snatch" grip.

53

KNOCK, KNOCK.

Who's there?

EMOM.

EMOM who?

E-MOM-ent of silence for our sore muscles, please.

54

WHY DID THE CROSSFITTER TAKE UP GARDENING?

They wanted to "cultivate" their muscles.

55

HOW MANY CROSSFITTERS DOES IT TAKE TO CHANGE A LIGHTBULB?

Just one, but they'll count it as a rep.

56

CROSSFIT IS LIKE A ROLLERCOASTER:

You scream, you cry, and you wonder why you paid for the experience.

57

WHY DO CROSSFITTERS EXCEL AT CROSSWORD PUZZLES?

They're experts at decoding acronyms.

58

CROSSFITTERS DON'T JUST "LIFT" WEIGHTS

They "raise" the bar.

59

YOU KNOW YOU'RE A CROSSFITTER

When the best part of your day is lying on the floor in a pool of sweat.

60

CROSSFIT IS LIKE A GAME OF RUSSIAN ROULETTE

Sometimes, you survive unscathed, and sometimes, you get a workout that feels like a bullet to the chest.

61

I THOUGHT I KNEW WHAT DEDICATION WAS

But then I met a CrossFitter who does double workouts on their rest days.

62

WHAT'S A CROSSFITTER'S FAVORITE BOOK?

"Fifty Shades of DOMS."

63

WHY DO CROSSFITTERS MAKE TERRIBLE THIEVES?

They can't resist the urge to "lift heavy" in public.

64

WHY DO CROSSFITTERS LOVE MATH?

They're always trying to find the perfect formula for gains.

65

YOU KNOW YOU'RE A CROSSFITTER

When your friends think you're speaking a foreign language every time you mention your workout.

66

CROSSFIT IS LIKE PLAYING WITH FIRE:

You never know when you'll get burned, but you keep coming back for more.

67

WHAT'S A CROSSFITTER'S FAVORITE MOVIE?

"Gone with the WOD."

68

KNOCK, KNOCK.

Who's there?

Rowing.

Rowing who?

Rowing through these workouts like there's no tomorrow!

69

A CROSSFITTER WAS HAVING A CONVERSATION WITH THEIR FRIEND WHO HAD RECENTLY STARTED CROSSFIT.

The friend said, "I heard CrossFit is like joining a cult, is that true?" The CrossFitter replied, "Absolutely not! We just have secret handshakes, rituals, and our own language. Now let's go work on our thrusters and kipping pull-ups."

70

WHY DO CROSSFITTERS LOVE LISTENING TO ROCK MUSIC?

It's the perfect soundtrack for their "rock hard" workouts.

71

A CROSSFITTER WENT ON A DATE AND COULDN'T STOP TALKING ABOUT THEIR GYM.

Their date finally asked, "Is there anything else you're interested in?" The CrossFitter paused and said, "Sure! I also love talking about my macros and meal prep."

72

I USED TO THINK I WAS GOOD AT MULTITASKING

But then I tried CrossFit and realized I can barely breathe and lift weights at the same time.

73

A CROSSFITTER WAS SHOWING OFF THEIR IMPRESSIVE COLLECTION OF WORKOUT SHOES TO A FRIEND.

The friend asked, "Why do you need so many shoes?" The CrossFitter replied, "Well, I have my lifting shoes, my running shoes, my rope climbing shoes, my box jump shoes, my burpee shoes, my rowing shoes... you get the idea. I need a shoe for every movement, so I'm always prepared!"

74

A CROSSFITTER WAS HAVING A CONVERSATION WITH THEIR PERSONAL TRAINER FRIEND WHEN THE TOPIC OF REST DAYS CAME UP.

The personal trainer asked, "So, what do you do on your rest days?" The CrossFitter replied, "Oh, you know, just the usual: active recovery, mobility work, and maybe a light 5K run. Rest is important, after all."

75

KNOCK, KNOCK.

Who's there?
PR.
PR who?
PR-epare yourself for a new personal record!

76

IF CROSSFITTERS RULED THE WORLD

There would be a law requiring everyone to wear weightlifting belts and knee sleeves at all times.

77

CROSSFIT:

Where the pain of your workout is only matched by your excitement for the next one.

78

A CROSSFITTER AND A SWIMMER WERE COMPARING THEIR WORKOUTS WHEN THE SWIMMER ASKED

"Don't you get bored doing the same exercises all the time?" The CrossFitter chuckled and said, "Bored? With constantly varied functional movements performed at high intensity? Never! Now let me tell you about the 12 different variations of burpees we did last week."

79

THEY SAY MISERY LOVES COMPANY

And that's why CrossFitters do their workouts together.

80

IN THE WORLD OF CROSSFIT

A "good time" is measured by how quickly you can collapse on the floor after a WOD.

81

WHY DO CROSSFITTERS LOVE GOING TO THE BEACH?

They get to show off their "ab-mirable" physiques.

82

HOW MANY CROSSFITTERS DOES IT TAKE TO CHANGE A TIRE?

None—they'd rather flip it.

83

A CROSSFITTER TRIED SETTING UP THEIR FRIEND WITH A FELLOW GYM MEMBER.

The friend asked, "What do they look like?" The CrossFitter responded, "Well, they have a great snatch, an impressive clean and jerk, and a killer deadlift." The friend shook their head and said, "I meant their face."

84

I LOVE CROSSFIT

But sometimes I wonder if my gym membership is just an expensive way to make myself cry in public.

85

YOU KNOW YOU'RE A CROSSFITTER

When you brag about your calluses and ripped hands as if they're trophies.

86

CROSSFIT

The only place where people complain about how much something hurts while paying for it to happen again tomorrow.

87

WHY DO CROSSFITTERS LOVE PIRATE MOVIES?

They can't resist a good "booty-building" workout.

88

CROSSFITTERS ARE SO DEDICATED

That they'll start measuring their laundry in reps and rounds.

89

YOU MIGHT BE A CROSSFITTER

If you're more concerned about your Fran time than your bedtime.

90

WHY DO CROSSFITTERS HAVE SUCH A GREAT SENSE OF HUMOR?

They need to find a way to laugh through the pain.

91

CROSSFIT

Turning fitness enthusiasts into masochists who love a good whipping from a jump rope.

92

WHY DID THE CROSSFITTER GO TO A STRIP CLUB?

They heard it was a great place to practice their muscle-ups.

93

HOW MANY CROSSFITTERS DOES IT TAKE TO SCREW IN A LIGHTBULB?

Just one, but they have to do it while standing on a box and wearing nothing but their favorite gym shorts.

94

YOU KNOW YOU'RE A CROSSFITTER

When you're just as comfortable talking about your snatch technique as you are about your latest Netflix binge.

95

CROSSFIT IS LIKE A SEXY DOMINATRIX

It'll push you to your limits, leaving you sore and begging for more.

96

IF CROSSFITTERS HAD THEIR WAY

Tinder profiles would only list Fran times and max deadlifts.

97

A CROSSFITTER WHO CAN'T DO DOUBLE UNDERS

Is like a chef who can't boil water—they're in the wrong profession.

98

WHY DID THE CROSSFITTER BREAK UP WITH THEIR PARTNER?

They realized they weren't a good "fit."

99

YOU KNOW YOU'RE A CROSSFITTER

When you spend more on workout clothes than you do on regular clothes.

100

CROSSFIT IS LIKE AN EX

You keep going back, even though it hurts, and you know you'll regret it in the morning.

Copyright © 2023 by The 100 Book Club – www.100bookclub.com

All rights reserved.

No portion of this book may be reproduced in any form without written permission from the publisher or author, except as permitted by copyright law.

Printed in Great Britain
by Amazon